The Power of SUBMISSION

Creating the spiritual for God to operate and manifest His power and glory

Dr David Oronsaye

Published by
Filament Publishing Ltd
16 Croydon Road, Waddon, Croydon,
Surrey, CR0 4PA, United Kingdom
Telephone +44 (0)20 8688 2598
Fax +44 (0)20 7183 7186
www.filamentpublishing.com
info@filamentpublishing.com

© 2015 Dr. David Oronsaye
ISBN 978-1-910125-89-2

The right of Dr. David Oronsaye to be identified as the author of this work has been asserted by him in accordance with the Designs and Copyright Act 1988.

Printed by IngramSpark

All rights reserved.
No portion of this work may be copied in any way without the prior written permission of the publisher.

All Scripture quotations are from the New King James Version of the Bible, except otherwise stated.

DEDICATION

I dedicate this book to my Inspirer, Leader and Teacher: the Holy Spirit.

ABOUT THE AUTHOR

Rev. Dr David Oronsaye is a prophet to the nations, a seasoned preacher with a mandate to stir up the body the body of Christ for the end time move of God. He is the general overseers of All Nations Christian Centre international. He is a husband and a father to four daughters and author of several inspirational books.

CONTENTS

PREFACE — 7

CHAPTER ONE — 9
Understanding Submission

CHAPTER TWO — 19
The Power of Submission in Jesus Christ

CHAPTER THREE — 29
The Power of Submission in the Early Church

CHAPTER FOUR — 41
The Power of Submission in the Prodigal Son

CHAPTER FIVE — 49
The Power of Submission in the Roman Centurion

CHAPTER SIX — 57
The Power of Submission in Elisha

CHAPTER SEVEN — 63
The Power of Submission in Joseph

CHAPTER EIGHT — 71
The Power of Submission in David

CHAPTER NINE — 81
The Power of Submission in Naaman

CHAPTER TEN — 87
The Power of Submission in Noah

PREFACE

Where there is submission there is order, and where there is order there is progress, success, advancement, increase, and joy. On the contrary, where there is no submission there is rebellion and where there is rebellion there is division and where there is division, there will be chaos, confusion, stagnation, corruption and sorrow. While submission creates a spiritual atmosphere for God to operate and manifest His power and glory, rebellion sets the foundation for the devil to operate, build and establish his dominion.

Many believers today pray and fast but all in vain to resist the devil, to break his hold off their lives, and overthrow him in their lives, homes, and businesses. They bind the devil continually but he refuses to be bound; they resist him steadfastly but he refuses to flee from them, and the more they pray against the devil, the more he afflicts, torments and oppresses them. This is so because the foundation of the devil's throne in their lives, homes and businesses has not been destroyed. Rebellion to God and God-appointed authorities is the sure and solid foundation of the devil's throne in any life, home, ministry, business, community, city or nation. The only potent instrument that can destroy that evil foundation is perfect submission to God and God-appointed authorities. When you are under God's authority you will wield His authority, and when you resist the devil and he will flee from you. **"Therefore submit to God. Resist the devil and he will flee from you."** (Jam. 4:7).

It is lack of submission in the home that keeps the devil in place. It is lack of submission in the Church that creates the atmosphere for the devil to operate and manifest. It is lack of submission in our cities that makes the demons to go on rampage. What a great power and authority the Church will wield in the world if she perfectly submits to her head – Jesus Christ.

What a great power and authority the husband will wield and great blessings he will attract to his family if he perfectly submits to his head – Jesus Christ, and the wife if she perfectly submits to her husband in all things, and the children if they perfectly submit to their parents in the Lord. This book is indeed a timely help from God to open your eyes of understanding to the powerful forces and blessings that emanate from a life of submission to God and God-appointed authorities. It is also a divine empowerment for you to break, overthrow and destroy the strong foundation of the devil's throne put in place by rebellion in your life, home, ministry or business.

CHAPTER ONE

UNDERSTANDING SUBMISSION

Submission is the acknowledgement of the legitimacy of the power of one's superior or superiors. It implies a willingness to yield or surrender to somebody. It also implies a yielding to the judgement or control of a recognized superior or authority. It is a condition of being submissive, humble or compliant. It speaks of being accountable or answerable to somebody; acquiescence, capitulation, compliance, obedience or meekness.

True submission begins with you acknowledging the headship or authority of Jesus Christ and surrendering your whole life to him. Jesus Christ is the King of kings and the Lord of lords. He is the ultimate ruler of the universe and all authorities proceed from him. The Scripture declares about Jesus:

> *"He is the image of the invisible God, the firstborn over all creation. For by Him all things were created that are in heaven and that are on earth, visible and invisible, whether thrones or dominions or principalities or powers. All things were created through Him and for Him. And He is before all things, and in Him all things consist. And He is the head of the body, the church, who is the beginning,*

> *the firstborn from the dead, that in all things He may have the preeminence." (Col. 1:15-18).*

Submission implies knowing your place in the body of Christ and abiding in your place. It means you recognize that Jesus is the head of the church and you are a member of his body, specially placed in a special position to fulfil a special role in the body of Christ.

> *"For as the body is one and has many members, but all the members of that one body, being many, are one body, so also is Christ. For by one Spirit we were all baptized into one body-- whether Jews or Greeks, whether slaves or free-- and have all been made to drink into one Spirit. For in fact the body is not one member but many." (1 Cor. 12:12-14).*

> *"Now you are the body of Christ, and members individually." (1 Cor. 12:27).*

One of the major causes of division and confusion in the body of Christ today is that many members of the body are not staying in their divine placement in the body. Rather than staying where the Spirit of God has divinely put them under the head in the body, they roam about in disobedience and in arrogance, and claiming and camouflaging to be what they are not. No wonder, the devil is not afraid of them and does not flee when they resist him. Until you submit yourself to God – serve Him in love and humility where He has put you, you cannot put devil to flight (Jam. 4:7). Until you begin to walk in obedience to God you cannot walk in His power and blessings. For **"God sets the solitary in families; He brings out those who are bound into prosperity; But the rebellious dwell in a dry land" (Psa. 68:6).**

It is lack of submission to God – rebellion and disobedience to His words and commandments that has confined many believers to a dry land – where they are famishing with hunger and thirst, destitute of favour of God and men. The Church today is not experiencing the full blessings of God and manifestations of the Spirit not because of the power of the devil or his demons, but primarily because of rebellion to God's word. When you refuse to obey God, nothing God created will obey you. When you don't submit to the word, the world will not submit to you. When you don't submit to God-ordained authority, nobody will submit to your authority. You don't earn the right to be a leader until you have humbled yourself to be led. When you submit to God and godly leadership, God will put all things under your feet.

Unity of the body flows from submission of the members of the body to the instructions and commands from the head. But when orders or commands from the body are rejected and refused, the body will be thrown into confusion as every member of the body will begin to function independently and contrarily to one another. This is what the body of Christ today is experiencing due to disregard and disobedience to divine commands and instructions from Jesus – our head. Unity is the colour of God, and this must also be the colour of the Church. God the Father, God the Son and God the Holy Spirit are perfectly united and submissive to one another. God the Son came into the world to do the will of God the Father. He did not glorify Himself but His Father. Jesus humbly declared, *"I can of Myself do nothing. As I hear, I judge; and My judgment is righteous, because I do not seek My own will but the will of the Father who sent Me. "If I bear witness of Myself, My witness is not true." (John 5:30-31).* The Holy Spirit also came not to speak of Himself but to speak of Jesus and glorify Him. Jesus said of the Holy Spirit: *"However, when He, the Spirit of truth, has come, He will guide you into all truth; for He will not speak on His own authority, but whatever He hears He will speak; and He will tell you things to come. "He will glorify Me, for He will take of what is Mine and declare it to you. (John 16:13-14).*

God's earnest desire for the Church today is unity (John 17:20-21). Division, disunity or disharmony which is the fruit of lack of submission or rebellion is Satan's identity and colour. God is calling the Church today to manifest His true colour to the world. Enough of parading ourselves in Satan's uniform and mark of disunity. But until submission is in place, unity is not attainable. Until we understand what submission is, we cannot experience true love and unity in the body of

Christ. Where God is not in charge, Satan will take over and manifest his nature of division and confusion.

When the body is disconnected from the head, it loses its life and dies. So also when any member of the body is severed and separated from the body, it withers and dies. It is submission to God that guarantees a continuous flow of God's life. Where there is no more submission to God, life will cease and death will take over. It is only as you walk in submission and obedience to God's word that your life is secured in Christ. It is also as you stay and operate in your divine place in the body of Christ that you will continue to enjoy the life of Christ. While submission is life, rebellion is death. The moment you begin to ignore, disregard or disobey God and the human authority He has placed over you, you will begin to die and wither. When the wife disrespects and disconnects herself from her husband (the head of the home), she will begin to wither and die spiritually until she repents and returns to her place under the headship of her husband. The Bible warns:

> *"I am the true vine, and My Father is the vinedresser." Every branch in Me that does not bear fruit He takes away; and every branch that bears fruit He prunes, that it may bear more fruit. "You are already clean because of the word which I have spoken to you. "Abide in Me, and I in you. As the branch cannot bear fruit of itself, unless it abides in the vine, neither can you,*

unless you abide in Me. "I am the vine, you are the branches. He who abides in Me, and I in him, bears much fruit; for without Me you can do nothing. "If anyone does not abide in Me, he is cast out as a branch and is withered; and they gather them and throw them into the fire, and they are burned." (John 15:1-6).

Though God is the Ultimate ruler of the universe, yet He shares His rule and authority with men. He appoints and places men and women in various positions of leadership and authority as it pleases Him. God has set the man as the head of the home and all the members of the home – wife and children must obey and submit to him. God has also set in the Church, apostles, prophets, pastors, evangelists and teachers as His representatives, and members of the church must obey them. You also have the Prime Ministers, Presidents, Head of States, Kings and Queens placed in positions of authority over nations and cities, and they must be respected and obeyed. You have your bosses in the office to which you are accountable. Watch it! Whenever you disobey and rebel against those in authority, you are setting yourself against the God who put them there. The Scripture admonishes:

"Let every soul be subject to the governing authorities. For there is no authority except from God, and the authorities that exist are appointed by God. Therefore whoever resists the authority

resists the ordinance of God, and those who resist will bring judgment on themselves. For rulers are not a terror to good works, but to evil. Do you want to be unafraid of the authority? Do what is good, and you will have praise from the same. For he is God's minister to you for good. But if you do evil, be afraid; for he does not bear the sword in vain; for he is God's minister, an avenger to execute wrath on him who practices evil. Therefore you must be subject, not only because of wrath but also for conscience' sake. For because of this you also pay taxes, for they are God's ministers attending continually to this very thing. Render therefore to all their due: taxes to whom taxes are due, customs to whom customs, fear to whom fear, honour to whom honour." (Romans 13:1-7).

Whoever resists the authority God has appointed whether at home, in the church, in the school, office or in a nation does not resist men but God and His ordinance. Be careful! When you disrespect, disregard or disobey your husband, leaders in the church, your boss in the office or government; you have made yourself an enemy of God and have put yourself under His judgment. Any hardness, rebellion or insult to those in authority is to God and God will judge it.

Also, the above Scripture warns that those in authority bear the sword in their hands, and it is therefore self-suicidal to rise up against your husband, parents, boss or pastor. Rebellion carries a death penalty as far as God is concerned. From Genesis to Revelation, every rebellion is crushed and punished by God and resulted in death. When Absalom rose up and set himself against his father – David, without the help of any man, he was hanged between heaven and earth by divine hand as a warning against rebellion. The Scripture reveals:

> *"Then Absalom met the servants of David. Absalom rode on a mule. The mule went under the thick boughs of a great terebinth tree, and his head caught in the terebinth; so he was left hanging between heaven and earth. And the mule which was under him went on." (2 Samuel 18:9).*

God neither overlooks nor treats lightly rebellion to His appointed authorities. When you choose the path of disobedience and rebellion to God and those He put in authorities, you have chosen the path of swift destruction. A life of rebellion is a life sentence to sorrow, poverty and disgrace. When you disgrace your parents, husband, pastor or boss; you are setting the stage of public disgrace and ridicule for yourself. Absalom set out to resist and disgrace his father but he ended up in a public disgrace, ridicule and death – he was left hanging between heaven and earth. That is always the reward, the end or fruit of lack of submission or rebellion to authority.

However, anyone who chooses the path of submission is on the path of greatness, glory and goodness. Submission is a great ladder to great heights in life. David followed the path of submission in his relationship with King Saul and it landed him on the exalted throne of Israel. Even when Saul treated him unfairly and sought after his life, David chose not to insult, disgrace or resist Saul. All through his life, David treated Saul as God's anointed — as he would treat God Himself, with love, honour and humility. He would not raise his hand or sword against him even when Saul was fast asleep and vulnerable. What a man of wisdom David was! No wonder God brought him from the field to the palace, from the back-side of life to the frontline, from the bottom of his family to be the first in the nation of Israel. God loved David greatly for his perfect submission to Him and men in authority, He made an everlasting covenant with him and gave him the honour of having Jesus come from his family line, and Jesus Christ is even called the Son of David (1 Samuel 26:1-25, Matthew 1:1-16).

Beloved, God is calling you today to a life of perfect submission and obedience to His word and whoever He puts in authority. Submission is a major key to your success, breakthrough and progress in life. Without it, you will only continue to wander aimlessly in the dry land. Your destiny in Christ is secured and fulfilled only in the path of submission. Choose to follow the path of submission, humility and obedience for that is the good path that leads to abundant life in Christ. Submission neither reduces nor subtracts from a man but rather it will add great values and flavours to your life. Submission is a lifter – when you humble yourself in the sight of the Lord and those in authority, you will be lifted up (James 4:10). God only gives grace – power or oil of favour, success, joy and prosperity to the humble. On the contrary, God resists and fights and dethrones the proud, arrogant, unruly and rebellious. So, choose submission today and steps on your ladder to the topmost top in life.

Believers in Christ are called to a life of submission which is the life of Christ and this is characterized by:

1. Submission to God – His word and the Holy Spirit (Gen. 16:9, Jam. 4:7, 2Chron. 30:8, Heb. 12:9)
2. Submission to your husband, and husband must love and honour his wife (1Pet. 3: 1-7)
3. Submission to your spiritual leader, pastor or leader of your church organization (1Pet. 5:5-9)
4. Submission to one another (1Pet. 5:5-9)
5. Submission to your parents (Eph. 6:1-3)
6. Submission to the government (1Pet. 2:13-17)
7. Submission to your boss (1Pet. 2:18-25

CHAPTER TWO

THE POWER OF SUBMISSION IN JESUS CHRIST

Jesus Christ is the embodiment of perfect submission. He is our perfect model of submission to the will and plan of God. In Jesus Christ, the divinity submitted to the humanity for the purpose of our redemption. His incarnation was submission in action. His obedience to His earthly parents was submission par excellence, and baptism by John the Baptist was an act of submission. Jesus Christ lived and taught submission to God and appointed authority. In Jesus Christ, the power and blessings of submission are clearly evident. Jesus' life clearly demonstrated the beauty and glory of submission. We can not be like Christ, experience and demonstrate His power until we follow His footsteps in submission.

JESUS' SUBMISSION TO HIS HEAVENLY FATHER

"Let this mind be in you which was also in Christ Jesus, who, being in the form of God, did not consider it robbery to be equal with God, but made Himself of no reputation, taking the form of a bondservant, and coming in the likeness of men. And being found in appearance as a man, He humbled Himself and

became obedient to the point of death, even the death of the cross. Therefore God also has highly exalted Him and given Him the name which is above every name, that at the name of Jesus every knee should bow, of those in heaven, and of those on earth, and of those under the earth, and that every tongue should confess that Jesus Christ is Lord, to the glory of God the Father." (Philippians 2:5-11).

Jesus Christ is God – the second person in the Holy trinity. He was the Word that was with God –the Father at the beginning and all things were made through Him, and without Him nothing was made that was made (John 1:1-2). But in perfect submission to God and His plan and purpose of redemption for mankind, Jesus – the Word became flesh. His incarnation was indeed an expression of submission. He had to empty Himself of His divine power, might, wisdom, beauty and glory as God. Imagine the creator coming in the form of a servant! That was a great humiliation, but a real example of submission.

Not only did Jesus abandoned His throne in heaven and emptied Himself of all His divine attributes and virtues as God in submission to His Father's plan and purpose of salvation of mankind, while on earth, He neither said nor did anything independently of His heavenly Father. He did nothing except what His Father commanded Him to do; He sought not His own will or glory but that of His Father; His doctrines, teachings and words were not His own but that of His Father who sent Him. What a lifestyle of submission Jesus left behind for us to follow. He loudly, clearly and humbly declared:

> *"Then Jesus answered and said to them, "Most assuredly, I say to you, the Son can do nothing of Himself, but what He sees the Father do; for whatever He does, the Son also does in like manner." (John 5:19).*
>
> *"I can of Myself do nothing. As I hear, I judge; and My judgment is righteous, because I do not seek My own will but the will of the Father who sent Me. "If I bear witness of Myself, My witness is not true." (John 5:30-31).*
>
> *"Jesus answered them and said, "My doctrine is not Mine, but His who sent Me. "If anyone wants to do His will, he shall know concerning the doctrine, whether it is from God or whether I speak on My own authority. "He who speaks from himself seeks his own glory; but He who seeks the glory of the One who sent Him is true, and no unrighteousness is in Him." (John 7:16-18).*
>
> *"Then Jesus said to them, "When you lift up the Son of Man, then you will know that I am He, and that I do nothing of Myself; but as My Father*

taught Me, I speak these things. "And He who sent Me is with Me. The Father has not left Me alone, for I always do those things that please Him." (John 8:28-29).

While on the earth, as a result of His perfect submission to the will of God – His Father, Jesus Christ enjoyed awesome divine presence and power. His Father never left nor forsook Him. God was pleased to identify with Him and introduce Him to all as His beloved Son in whom He is well pleased. At Jordan, during His water baptism and on the Mount of Transfiguration, God – the Father proudly and loudly thundered from heaven, **"This is My beloved Son, in whom I am well pleased. Hear Him!" (Matth. 17:5)**. All creations were commanded by God to submit to Jesus and hear Him because He submitted to God and heard Him. Jesus' words carried God's power and never returned to Him void; He was filled with the Holy Spirit without measure; God's presence and power was always present while He taught and preached, to heal the sick and deliver the captives and the oppressed; He cast out demons by His words and raised the dead. He enjoyed all these blessings not because He was God on the earth but because He was a Son who perfectly submitted to His Heavenly father.

Ultimately, because Jesus chose the path and life of submission, His Father did not allow Him to see corruption in the grave. After three days in the grave, He was raised from the dead by the glory of the Father, and was highly exalted and honoured by His Father, and was given the name that is above every name. *"Therefore God also has highly exalted Him and given Him the name which is above every name, that at the name of Jesus every knee should bow, of those in heaven, and of those on earth, and of those under the earth, and that every tongue should confess that Jesus Christ is Lord, to the glory of God the Father." (Phil. 2:9-11).*

Beloved, if you also walk in Jesus' footsteps of submission, you will also experience and enjoy God's presence and power. The Church today is void of God's presence, power and glory because of rebellion and disobedience to God. God does not identify with rebellious and disobedient people. He is only well-pleased in those who perfectly surrender to His perfect will, plan and purpose. God cannot be found in the place of chaos and confusion created by rebellion as we have in our churches and nations today. Though Jesus neither testified nor glorified Himself when He was in the world, yet the Father sought every occasion to introduce and glorify Him. Unfortunately, many servants of God today seek every occasion to testify of themselves, project themselves, and boast, yet they are not glorified, honoured and exalted by God. The path of submission is the path of glory and honour, you cannot choose and follow that path and not experience divine glory, honour, favour and exaltation.

JESUS' SUBMISSION TO HIS EARTHLY PARENTS

"His parents went to Jerusalem every year at the Feast of the Passover. And when He was twelve years old, they went up to Jerusalem according to the custom of the feast. When they had finished the days, as they returned, the Boy Jesus lingered behind in Jerusalem. And Joseph and His mother did not know it; but supposing Him to have been in the company, they went a day's journey, and sought Him among their relatives and acquaintances. So when they did not find Him, they returned to Jerusalem, seeking Him. Now so it was that after three days they found Him in the temple, sitting in the midst of the teachers, both listening to them and asking them questions. And all who heard Him were astonished at His understanding and answers. So when they saw Him, they were amazed; and His mother said to Him, "Son, why have You done this to us? Look, Your father and I have sought You anxiously." And He said to them, "Why did you seek Me? Did you not know that I must be about My Father's business?" But they did not understand the statement which He spoke to them. Then He went down with them and came to Nazareth, and was subject to them, but His mother kept all these things in her heart. And Jesus increased in wisdom and stature, and in favour with God and men." (Luke 2:41-52).

Jesus did not only submit to His Heavenly father, He also perfectly submitted to His earthly parents as presented in the above passage. Though He was God and on God's mission, Jesus acknowledged the authority of His parents over Him as a young boy. He obeyed, respected and listened to them. He neither disregarded nor insulted them publicly or privately. He perfectly followed their instructions as they did not conflict with that of God. He submitted to their training in righteousness. He chose not to follow His own way as a young boy but that which His parents showed Him – the way of the fear of the Lord. He followed them to the Temple in Jerusalem to worship and serve God, and though He would have loved to stay behind many days to listen and ask questions from the teachers of the Law, He followed His parents to Nazareth and was subject to them. What a display of submission to divine order and authority!

What followed Jesus' respect and submission to God's divine order and authority in the home was divine increase in wisdom, stature and favour with God and men. Submission always results in supernatural increase. You can not submit to God, your parents and God's set order and authority and not go forward in life. Submission is a divine key that unlocks the doors of favour, progress and promotion. Many children today are not going forward in their academic and careers because of rebellion and disobedience to their parents, guardians and teachers. The spirit of submission is the spirit of wisdom. You cannot be walking in the path of submission and be a dullard. You cannot be under God's divine order and still be under heavy yokes of oppression, poverty, stagnation or retrogression. This is absolutely impossible. Submission breaks the yoke of stagnation. It sets you free to increase in stature, finances, favour, wisdom and grace. What great blessings we miss due to our disregard for God's divine order and appointed authority.

JESUS' SUBMISSION TO JOHN THE BAPTIST

"Then Jesus came from Galilee to John at the Jordan to be baptized by him. And John tried to prevent Him, saying, "I need to be baptized by You, and are You coming to me?" But Jesus answered and said to him, "Permit it to be so now, for thus it is fitting for us to fulfill all righteousness." Then he allowed Him. When He had been baptized, Jesus came up immediately from the water; and behold, the heavens were opened to Him, and He saw the Spirit of God descending like a dove and alighting upon Him. And suddenly a voice came from heaven, saying, "This is My beloved Son, in whom I am well pleased." (Matthew 3:13-17).

In Jesus, divinity submitted to humanity. Jesus (God - the Son) submitted to John the Baptist (a mortal man) according to divine order. John the Baptist was sent ahead of Jesus' arrival as a herald or fore-runner of His coming. Though, John protested, recognizing the superiority of Christ's authority and ministry, yet Jesus insisted on doing what was right and fitting according to God's order. By this act, Jesus affirmed the call and ministry of John the Baptist, and also showed His respect for the authority God has put in place. John was God-appointed authority in the days of Jesus to announce the coming arrival of God's kingdom and call the nation of Israel to repentance. All the people recognized and respected his ministry and authority. ***"Then Jerusalem, all Judea, and all the region around the Jordan went out to him and were baptized by him in the Jordan, confessing their sins." (Matthew 3:5-6).*** So, if Jesus chose not to come to John for baptism at Jordan, He would be despising and disregarding God-set authority in His days. Though, Jesus was the Light and the arrival of the Kingdom of Heaven on earth that John came to introduce, yet He came to John to be baptized and thus submitting to God's authority that John represented at that time.

In response to Jesus' submission to His Father's authority and order that John represented, the heavens were opened to Him; the Holy Spirit like a dove descended upon Him; and God attested to His sonship before all men. What a blessing that follows submission. Many children of God today operate under a closed heaven because of disobedience to God and rebellion to God-set order and authority in the home, church, organization, and nation. While submission opens the heavens and attracts a heavy downpour of God's blessings, rebellion always shuts the heavens. When the Church walks in submission to God, God will pour out His Spirit upon all the flesh; when a servant of God submits to God and has regard for constituted and delegated authority, God will attest to, certify and bear witness to his call and ministry with great signs and wonders.

Beloved, wisdom is calling you today to sit down now and carefully examine your life and way. Do you regard and submit to God-set authority in your home? How do you treat your husband? Is it with contempt or respect? How do you treat your wife and children? How do you treat your pastor or spiritual leaders? How do you treat your boss in the office? Do you have regard for the traffic rules? Do you abide by the rules of the nation where you live? Do you respect divine order and hierarchy? Now is the time to repent and begin to do what is right and fitting in the sight of God. When rebellion shuts your heavens, prayer and fasting alone cannot open them, you must begin to walk in submission. God is calling you today to a life of submission so that your heavens may open and pour you out great blessings. Anyone who walks in submission walks under open heavens but anyone who walks in rebellion walks under closed heavens. What is your choice today?

CHAPTER THREE

THE POWER OF SUBMISSION IN THE EARLY CHURCH

The Church that was born on the day of Pentecost was a Church where order and submission reigned. The Apostles – the human leadership of the Church were men who understood the power of submission. They saw and learned submission in Jesus Christ – their master. From the point of their call to their departure from this world, they denied themselves, took their crosses and followed closely after Jesus. They yielded absolutely to the Lord. They forsook all to follow Him and never went back except the son of perdition. The boldly declared: *"See, we have left all and followed You." (Mark 10:28).* Even when given the opportunity to go back from following the Lord, they responded: *"Lord, to whom shall we go?" (John 6:68).*

The apostles did not only follow and serve the Lord in His presence; they remained faithful, obedient and submissive to Him even when He had ascended to heaven. In perfect obedience to the Lord's command, they went up into the upper room and waited for several days for the fulfillment of the Lord's promise – the outpouring of the Holy Spirit (Acts 1&2). After receiving the divine enablement, they went out and preached everywhere as commanded by the Lord Jesus Christ.

When Peter and John were arrested after the healing of the lame man at the gate of the temple called Beautiful and threatened and forbidden by the rulers and elders of Israel to speak or teach in the name of Jesus, they responded:

> *"But Peter and John answered and said to them, "Whether it is right in the sight of God to listen to you more than to God, you judge. "For we cannot but speak the things which we have seen and heard." (Acts 4:19-20).*

Even in the face of threat, imprisonment, suffering and opposition, the early apostles chose not to disobey the Lord. They gave themselves continually to prayer and the ministry of the word as commanded by the Lord. When imprisoned and challenged by the council, they re-stated their commitment and loyalty to the Lord:

> *"But Peter and the other apostles answered and said: "We ought to obey God rather than men. (Acts 5:29).*

It was not only the apostles that were obedient to the Lord's command but the entire Church. Submission is like the precious oil upon the head, running down on the body. When the husband – the leader or head of the home submits to God, the wife and children will follow his example and submit to the Lord, and there will be order in the home which will attract God and open the heavens upon the home. When the pastor or spiritual leader in the church walks in perfect obedience to the word of God, it will definitely flows to the members, for submission is like the oil and it can flow. The Church today is in a state of confusion because of lack of order and submission and this begins with the rebellion of the leaders to the Spirit of God.

Like her leaders, the early Church walked in obedience and unity. They continued steadfastly in the apostles' doctrine and fellowship, in the breaking of bread, and in prayers (Acts 2:42). Those who were possessors of lands or houses sold them and brought the proceeds of the things that were sold, and laid them at the apostles' feet (Acts 4:34-37). **"Now all who believed were together, and had all things in common, and sold their possessions and goods, and divided them among all, as anyone had need. So continuing daily with one accord in the temple, and breaking bread from house to house, they ate their food with gladness and simplicity of heart, praising God and having favor with all the people. And the Lord added to the church daily those who were being saved." (Acts 2:44-47).** What a life of total submission to God and the leadership He has put in place! This is the urgent need of the 21st century Church. To maintain and sustain order and prevent confusion, seven deacons were chosen and appointed to oversee daily distributions to the poor and widows (Acts 6:1-7).

Though full of faith and the Holy Spirit, the deacons, especially Stephen and Philip did not compete with the apostles. They respected them and submitted to their authority. They discharged faithfully their given duties. Even when they were all scattered throughout the land by persecution, no one usurped the power and role of the apostles. When Philip went to Samaria to preach, the apostles were sent for to pray for them that they might receive the Holy Spirit (Acts 8:14-17). All evangelists and missionaries remained connected and subjected to the apostles in Jerusalem. Not even the force of opposition or persecution could break the bond of unity in the early Church. Though physically scattered, they were united in the spirit because they continued to submit to God-appointed leadership and authority.

Sadly, in the Church today, there is no respect or regard for God-appointed leadership. The deacons envy the pastors and the evangelists compete with the pastors. Everybody wants to become an overseer and be self-independent. This is the cause of many breakaways in our churches today. Many new churches are springing up daily, not out of a genuine call or divine instruction but out of rebellion. Nobody wants to be under anybody. Everybody wants to be on his own, be his own apostle, prophet or pastor. This is why the Church today unlike the early Church is weak, powerless and without much influence or impact. May the Lord visit us again and bind us together, in Jesus' name.

THE BLESSINGS OF SUBMISSION IN THE EARLY CHURCH

The book of Acts gives a vivid account of the power, beauty, glory and blessings that emanate from the lifestyles of order and submission of the early apostles of Christ and the Church.

1.   ATTRACTION:

Submission paved the way, created the spiritual atmosphere, and set the platform for the Holy Spirit to come upon the 120 Disciples of Christ in the upper room on the day of Pentecost. First, they were there in obedience to Jesus' instruction and command (Luke 2:48-49). They tarried for several days waiting for the Lord to fulfil His promise. *"These all continued with one accord in prayer and supplication ... and in those days Peter stood up in the midst of the disciples..." (Acts 1:14-25)*. Second, Peter was acknowledged, respected and obeyed as the leader. All the rest of the disciples agreed with what he said and submitted to his leadership. When their submission was in place, the Holy Spirit came upon them. They all were filled with the Holy Spirit and spoke with other tongues as the Spirit gave them utterance. That attracted every man from every nation under heaven who was in Jerusalem. They all were amazed and marveled (Acts 2:1-12). And out of the multitudes that were attracted, three thousand souls were saved and added to the disciples.

Submission is like a magnet that attracts men. Where there is law and order and discipline and submission, people will flow there. In the world today, people flee from nations where there is chaos, war and confusion to places where there is order. Rebellion which breeds confusion and corruption always repel people. Unlike the early Church which attracted people, the Church today is repelling people from Christ because of lack of order and submission in the Church.

2.   SUPERNATURAL ACTS:

As the early Church continued in perfect submission to the Lord and steadfastly in the apostles' doctrine and fellowship, in breaking of bread and prayers, great fear came upon every soul and many wonders and signs were done through the apostles (Acts 2:42-43). The Bible testifies that *"that they brought the sick out into the streets and laid them on beds and couches, that at least the shadow of Peter passing by might fall on some of them. Also a multitude gathered from the surrounding cities to Jerusalem, bringing sick people and those who were tormented by unclean spirits, and they were all healed." (Acts 5:15-16).*

Submission creates a right spiritual atmosphere for the birth of miracles, signs and wonders. God only works and manifests where there is order and submission to His words and appointed-authority. Where there is confusion, disharmony and corruption born out of rebellion; God will be far away. No wonder in the Church today, in spite of many days of prayer and fasting, we see few supernatural acts of God. It is only in the place of submission that supernatural acts of God manifest. When the children of Israel followed the path of disobedience, God announced to them, *"For I will not go up in your midst, lest I consume you on the way, for you are stiff-necked people." (Exod. 33:3).* Whenever God shows up in the place where rebellion is reigning, it is to judge and punish the rebellious.

3. JOY:

Submission births unspeakable joy. The early Church experienced joy in the Holy Spirit. *"They ate their food with gladness and simplicity of heart..." (Acts 2:46)*. Not even beaten, suffering or imprisonment could take away their joy. When imprisoned and beaten, the apostles *"departed from the presence of the council, rejoicing that they were counted worthy to suffer shame for His name. And daily in the temple, and in every house, they did not cease teaching and preaching Jesus as the Christ." (Acts 5:41-42).* While in prison with feet fastened in the stocks and having being beaten with many stripes, Paul and Silas rose up at midnight to sing hymns to God, for being counted worthy to suffer for Christ's name (Acts 16:16-34). Only those who have perfectly submitted to God and His will, plan and purpose for their lives can rejoice in suffering, affliction and prison.

4. FAVOUR:

Submission also generates and provokes favour with God and men. The early Church walked in favour because they walked in submission to God and the apostles (Acts 2:47). God's favour does not answer to many days of fasting and prayer but perfect submission to God – obedience to His word and His appointed leadership or authority. Submission is the oil of favour. When the early Church had it, they were **"having favour with all people."** This is what many believers today lack. When you surrender absolutely to God, walking in His ways, doing His perfect will and submitting to His authority; God will command all people, even your enemies to favour and promote your cause in life.

5. RAPID GROWTH:

As the early Church continued steadfastly with one accord in the apostles' doctrine which of course was Christ's doctrine, the Lord added to the Church daily those who were being saved. ***"And believers were increasingly added to the Lord, multitudes of both men and women." (Acts 5:14).*** In the atmosphere of submission, the Church exploded in population. Submission produces rapid growth and speedy progress in any organization. Where there is order and discipline, speedy progress becomes inevitable. When the ministers of God in a church are perfectly in submission to God and the set man God has placed over the affairs of the church, the church will explode in population. When every staff is perfectly joined together with the manager or director of an organization, the organization will experience speedy growth, progress and expansion.

Many churches, businesses and organizations are not growing and flourishing today because of rebellion. Rebellion births division, division births confusion, and confusion births disintegration or decomposition. Watch it! Where ever rebellion takes root, there will be no productivity. When rebellion gets anywhere, it will scatter it. Rebellion is a destroyer, so have nothing to do with. However, submission ensures productivity. When everyone does what is expected of him, carries out his duties or responsibilities with all diligence and obey laid down rules, there will be good fruits of success, progress, increase and expansion. Submission eliminates conflicts and frictions, thus preserving much energy, time and resources that are often wasted in resolving conflicts. Submission creates a better working environment and initiates a better understanding and cooperation. Things work better, move faster and get better where there is order and submission.

6. GREAT POWER AND GREAT GRACE

Where there is great submission, there will be great power and great grace. As the apostles and the early Church walked in great submission to the will of God, great power and great grace came upon them all (Acts 4:33). The devil could not stand in their midst. When Satan filled the hearts of Ananias and Sapphira his wife to lie to the apostles, they were judged immediately (Acts 5:1-11). And great fear came upon all the church and upon all who heard these things. Rebellion always begins with deception. But when the leaders' obedience to God is complete, God will expose and judge every deception and rebellion (2 Cor. 10:5).

When persecution broke out against the early Church and they were all scattered through the regions of Judea and Samaria, Philip went down to Samaria with great power and grace of God and preached Christ to them. *"And the multitudes with one accord heeded the things spoken by Philip, hearing and seeing the miracles which he did. For unclean spirits, crying with a loud voice, came out of many who were possessed; and many who were paralyzed and lame were healed. And there was great joy in that city." (Acts 8:6-8).*

Where there is submission, great power and grace for great exploits is available to all. Submission empowers and brings out the values of every member of the Church or staff of an organization. Potentials are not wasted where there is order and submission but are rather developed and harnessed for God's glory and the profit of all. But where there is rebellion, there is confusion and great potentials are despised, wasted and buried.

7. PROSPERITY

Amazingly, in the early Church there was not anyone who lacked. That is the blessing that submission bestows. While they surrendered perfectly to the Lord, the Holy Spirit stirred up those who had possessions and goods to sell it and laid the proceeds at the feet of the apostles. Because of their obedience to God's command, the Church had abundance for the expansion of the gospel and welfare of her members (Acts 2:44-45, 4:32-37).

Many in today's Church are poor and destitute of basic necessities of life because many whom the Lord has tremendously blessed and prospered are not walking in submission to God's command. Holding back your tithes, offerings, gifts and donations to the work of God is an act of rebellion to God's express command in His word (Malachi 3:10, Prov. 3:9, 2 Cor. 9:6-8).

Poverty was cast out of the early Church by the power of submission. The rich laid their possessions and goods at the feet of the apostles. The early believers had all things in common. Neither did anyone say of the things he possessed was his own. The Church today can as well cast out lack and poverty out of her midst by teaching God's children how to hear and obey God's voice. Though the apostles never asked anyone to sell his house or possession and bring the proceeds as many preachers or prophets do today, yet, the people did it because they have been taught how to hear, recognize and obey the voice of God, and also the power and blessings of obedience to God. When believers today, like the early believers begin to hear and obey God's voice and command, the Church will prosper, attend to the welfare of the poor, widows and orphans, and have abundance for the spread of the gospel of Christ to all nations.

CHAPTER FOUR

THE POWER OF SUBMISSION IN THE PRODIGAL SON

"Then He said: "A certain man had two sons. "And the younger of them said to his father, 'Father, give me the portion of goods that falls to me.' So he divided to them his livelihood. "And not many days after, the younger son gathered all together, journeyed to a far country, and there wasted his possessions with prodigal living. "But when he had spent all, there arose a severe famine in that land, and he began to be in want. "Then he went and joined himself to a citizen of that country, and he sent him into his fields to feed swine. "And he would gladly have filled his stomach with the pods that the swine ate, and no one gave him anything. "But when he came to himself, he said, 'How many of my father's hired servants have bread enough and to spare, and I perish with hunger! 'I will arise and go to my father, and will say to him, "Father, I have sinned against heaven and before you, "and I am no longer worthy to be called your son. Make me like one of your hired servants."' "And he arose and came to his father. But when he was still a great way off, his father saw him and had compassion,

and ran and fell on his neck and kissed him. "And the son said to him, 'Father, I have sinned against heaven and in your sight, and am no longer worthy to be called your son.' "But the father said to his servants, 'Bring out the best robe and put it on him, and put a ring on his hand and sandals on his feet. 'And bring the fatted calf here and kill it, and let us eat and be merry; 'for this my son was dead and is alive again; he was lost and is found.' And they began to be merry." (Luke 15:11-24).

The account of the life of the prodigal son given in the above passage clearly depicts the blessings that submission to authority bestow and the woes that accompany rebellion to authority. While in submission under the authority of his father, the prodigal son had no lack. Under his father's authority, he had abundance, joy and favour, and wielded great influence and authority. He was celebrated, revered and blessed. He enjoyed life to the fullest. But his story and experience changed the moment he stepped out of his father's authority in rebellion.

THE WOES OF REBELLION IN THE PRODIGAL SON

The life of the prodigal son serves as a deterrent to a lifestyle of rebellion and disobedience. When he revolted against his father and moved far away from his authority and influence, the prodigal son began to experience the following:

1. SPIRITUAL DEATH:

While the prodigal son was in submission under his father's authority he enjoyed deep and intimate communion and fellowship with his father and family. In fellowship, he had the life and wisdom of his father imparted into his life. He was full of life and blessings of his father. But when rebellion set in, his communion with his father was broken and he became separated from his father and family. The flow of life and virtues to his life ceased and he was cut off from the fountain of life and grace. His father said of him, *"for this my son was dead..."*

Beloved, flee from rebellion! Rebellion is a terminator of life; it is a fast spiritual killer. Where ever rebellion goes, death immediately follows. Rebellion breaks fellowship and communion. It will cut you off from God and the Church of God. It will block the flow of good things to your life. When you refuse to cooperate with your pastor or your boss to pursue and fulfil the vision of the church or organization, you have cut yourself off from the flow of blessings. You cannot receive any blessing under the authority you do not submit to. Anointing always flows from the head down the body, so if you are not well connected to the body, it will not flow to you. When you are in rebellion, you are in the solitary place – in the realm of death. Now is the time to come out of that terrible place. Submission is the way out of the grave. When the prodigal son returned to his father and submitted to his authority, he came alive again. If you also return to the path of obedience and submission, you will come alive again. Your business, ministry, finances, marriage or whatever death has struck down will resurrect again and begin to live and abound in blessings.

2.   **WASTE and LOSS:**

"And not many days after, the younger son gathered all together, journeyed to a far country, and there wasted his possessions with prodigal living." (Luke 15:13).

Anyone who adopts the lifestyle of disobedience and rebellion cannot manage God's resources; you will only waste it. Rebellion is a waster. When your life is overtaken by rebellion, it will be wasted and reduced to nothing. While submission adds value to your life, rebellion will devalue you. Though you are gifted, talented and well qualified for a job, you will be fired or sacked when you fail to abide by the rules of the organization or submit to your boss. Nobody likes rebellious people around them. The pastor will despise your gifts or anointing, and call someone else to minister when you fail to submit under his authority. No wise leader or pastor will give his pulpit to a rebellious person. If you choose the path of disobedience to God's word and rebellion to His appointed authority, your potentials will be despised, discarded and devalued. The prodigal son did not only lose all his inheritance, he himself became lost in the wilderness of life. His father said of him, **"for this my son was lost and is found."**

3. CONFUSION:

Rebellion is the mother of confusion. It is the womb that nurtures and births chaos. When you submit to God's word and the human leader God has set over you, you will gain a heart of wisdom and understanding, and make wise decisions in life. Rebellion puts out the light of God in your heart and throws you into darkness. When the prodigal son chose to step out of his father's authority, he stepped into a thick darkness. Where ever you find rebellion, darkness will reign and where ever darkness reigns, people are thrown into confusion. While in rebellion, the prodigal son became a wanderer, without any vision, direction or provision. He became so confused that he lost his true identity, he considered himself to be a pig and compete for the pods that the swine ate. What a terrible price to pay for rebellion!

4. POVERTY:

Though the prodigal son began his journey in rebellion with great possessions, as he continued in the path, he began to diminish until he lost all and he began to be in want. Rebellion can never add to your life, it will only reduce you to nothing. The path of disobedience and rebellion only ends in poverty and wretchedness. When you walk in the ways of God, keep

His commandments and submit to His ordained authority; you will prosper. While the prodigal son was under his father's authority, doing his will and obeying his instructions; he was blessed – he lacked nothing good. He was fed with milk and honey and had many servants attending to his needs. But when he chose to follow his own evil ways, he ended up in poverty – in want of every good thing. He was taken from eating at the King's table to eating at the Pig's table. He became miserable, poor and wretched. The way out of poverty is total obedience to God's word.

> *"Now it shall come to pass, if you diligently obey the voice of the LORD your God, to observe carefully all His commandments which I command you today, that the LORD your God will set you high above all nations of the earth. "And all these blessings shall come upon you and overtake you, because you obey the voice of the LORD your God: "Blessed shall you be in the city, and blessed shall you be in the country. "Blessed shall be the fruit of your body, the produce of your ground and the increase of your herds, the increase of your cattle and the offspring of your flocks." (Deuteronomy 28:1-4).*

5. DISFAVOUR:

While in submission under his father's authority, the prodigal son enjoyed favour from all men. He had the oil of favour upon him, and where ever he went, doors of opportunities opened to him. People gave him what he did not even ask for. He was celebrated and highly respected. He was loved by all men. But rebellion robbed him of all those privileges. The oil of favour dried up; the doors of help and opportunities shut against him; and no one was willing to give him anything, even when he earnestly begged them. It was said of him: **"And he would gladly have filled his stomach with the pods that the swine ate, and no one gave him anything. (Luke 15:16).**

Beloved, as you can see from the account of the life of the prodigal son, rebellion is a robber, waster and destroyer. It will rob you of all your good inheritance in Christ; it will waste all your potentials, gifts or talents; and it will eventually destroy your life. However, like the prodigal son, if you make a U –turn today and repent and make necessary restitutions, you will recover all that you have lost.

When the prodigal son repented and returned under his father's authority, he walked back into glory, honour, favour, joy and prosperity. The dirty rag of shame and poverty was removed from him and replaced with the garment of glory and honour. He was restored to his seat at the king's table;

his ring – a symbol of authority was restored; and his servants were restored to him. All the people began to celebrate and honour and respect him. Like the father of the prodigal son, God is waiting for you to come back to your senses, repent and return under His authority. What are you still waiting for? Arise now, and go back to God and your spiritual leader, husband or boss to submit to their authority and you will experience total restoration.

CHAPTER FIVE

THE POWER OF SUBMISSION IN THE ROMAN CENTURION

"Now when Jesus had entered Capernaum, a centurion came to Him, pleading with Him, saying, "Lord, my servant is lying at home paralyzed, dreadfully tormented." And Jesus said to him, "I will come and heal him." The centurion answered and said, "Lord, I am not worthy that You should come under my roof. But only speak a word, and my servant will be healed. "For I also am a man under authority, having soldiers under me. And I say to this one, 'Go,' and he goes; and to another, 'Come,' and he comes; and to my servant, 'Do this,' and he does it." When Jesus heard it, He marvelled, and said to those who followed, "Assuredly, I say to you, I have not found such great faith, not even in Israel! "And I say to you that many will come from east and west, and sit down with Abraham, Isaac, and Jacob in the kingdom of heaven. "But the sons of the kingdom will be cast out into outer darkness. There will be weeping and gnashing of teeth." Then Jesus said to the centurion, "Go your way; and as you have believed, so let it be done for you." And his servant was healed that same hour." (Matthew 8:5-13).

A centurion is an officer in the Roman army (a captain in modern times) commanding hundred soldiers. His account shows that he is a man of great understanding. He clearly understood the meaning and power of submission to authority. He recognized, regarded and respected higher authority, and so enjoyed authority.

SUBMISSION IS BEING UNDER AUTHORITY

When the centurion's servant became very ill and paralyzed, because he was a humble and submissive servant, his master went to Jesus, pleading with Him to come and heal him. When you are submissive to your husband, he will gladly do anything for you. When you are submissive to your boss in the office, he will go to any extent to help you. When you are submissive to your pastor, he will be willing to pay any price to get you out of any unpleasant circumstances. Submission provokes devotion and unusual help. Whoever you are submissive to will be devoted to your welfare, and joyfully render any help you need to get out of your problems. Many believers today lack helpers because they are proud and arrogant, disobedient and rebellious to God and leaders God has placed over them.

The centurion introduced himself to Jesus Christ as a man under authority, having soldiers under him who obeyed his commands and carried out his orders. The centurion was an officer in the Roman army. He had superior officers over him that he respected, regarded and obeyed. He regularly received orders and instructions from them, and he was accountable to them. He was under their authority and that was why one hundred soldiers were placed under his own authority, too.

Submission is humility and compliance. It is operating under authority. It is being responsible and accountable to someone else. It is recognizing and acknowledging authority. The centurion recognized and submitted himself under Jesus' authority. Submission is you acknowledging and submitting to the authority of the Word of God. It is also acknowledging and submitting to the leadership of your husband in the home, your boss in the office and your pastor in the church. It is being available to do whatever you are instructed or commanded to do, and being accountable to them. It is not partial obedience to God's word. If you flee from fornication and adultery but participate in gossiping, backbiting and spreading of rumors and malicious lies in the church or in your office, then you are not submissive to God's word. *"For whoever shall keep the whole law, and yet stumble in one point, he is guilty of all. For He who said, "Do not commit adultery," also said, "Do not murder." Now if you do not commit adultery, but you do murder, you have become a transgressor of the law." (James 2:10-11).*

SUBMISSION IS GREAT FAITH

When Jesus saw the humility of the centurion and how he highly regarded and respected the power and authority of Jesus' word, Jesus marvelled, and said to those who followed Him, **"Assuredly, I say to you, I have not found such great faith, not even in Israel!" (Matt. 8:10).** When you submit to the authority of God's word, it means you have faith in God's word. When you obey God's command to honour Him with your tithes and offerings, it implies you have confidence and trust in God to fulfil His promises to open heavens above you and pour out upon you great blessings. When you submit to the leadership of your pastor or spiritual leader, it shows that you believe that he is truly called and sent of God, and that his vision is genuine. When you obey your boss in the office, you are saying that you believe in his leadership and the visions, goals or objectives of the company. When you respect and submit to the authority of your husband, it shows you accept and believe that he is the crown of your head and God's chosen man for you.

A person who does not submit to your godly authority does not value you or believe in your leadership. Rebellious people underestimate your worth and put you on the scale of devaluation. They will continually provoke and offend you. They will announce and rejoice at your night and darkness but not your light; your sin but not your righteousness; your disgrace but not your glory; and your fall but not your promotion or greatness. You are on your way to greatness and nothing can stop you in Jesus' name. Rebellion is a direct confrontation and message that your leadership skill, character, anointing, integrity and wisdom are in doubt and questionable. This is a serious matter.

For example, when a praise or worship minister refuses to submit to the pastor, there is no need for looking for the snake or demon troubling the church, you have already found and seen one. A wife who does not to submit to her husband is not a wife but a prostitute in marriage. Many women today are like this. Also, any man who does not honour his wife is a beast in the home. Not many men are husbands at home; most men are absentees in their marriage.

A person that refuses to submit to authority will create many enemies for you. He will slander you, and damage the organization's public image and reputation. When people refuse to submit to your authority, it weakens your authority and organization. Valuable time, energy and resources are wasted in resolving conflicts instead of focusing on organizational value and goal and development.

When people do not submit to your authority they will not celebrate your success, and they will not delight in your greatness. They are only ready to celebrate and rejoice at your failure and downfall. This will not be your portion, in Jesus' name. They will neither protect your interests nor keep your secrets. Their mission is to expose your weaknesses and nakedness. When you find out this kind of people in your organization, you should retire or fire them before they retire or fire you. If your house help refuses to submit to you and your wife, she is a satanic agent; fire him or her immediately. If your house help submits to your husband and refuses to submit to you (the wife); question your husband or else there will be civil war in your home.

Submission is refined behavioural oil. This oil is a must for any organization to function effectively with great ease. Unfortunately, there is little supply today, and demand is far higher than supply. Every wise employer is seeking for those who have this oil and virtue in them. Many problems arising in marriages, churches and private organizations are caused by rebellious people who lack the oil and grace of submission. A life of excellence carries this oil. People should not be judged or defined by their talk but rather by their character. Talk is cheap and easy but doing is expensive and tough.

SUBMISSION INITIATES HEALING AND DELIVERANCE

By the submission of the centurion's servant, his master was motivated to seek help from Jesus. By the submission of the centurion to the Lord Jesus Christ and His word, the power of God was release to deliver and heal the centurion's servant from the bondage of the demon of paralysis. Submission has power to initiate, activate and release God's healing and deliverance power. Many believers in our churches today remain sick, bound, tormented and afflicted by demons because they are living in rebellion and disobedience to God's word. When you don't submit under God's authority and that of the church leadership, you are the one hindering God's power from working in your life. The power of God only flows in the life of those who submit to God and His appointed authority.

The power of God flowed into the centurion's home and wrought great healing and deliverance because order and submission were found there. The centurion was a man under authority and his sick servant was also under authority. It is the authority that you submit to that will fight for you, lift you up, defend and protect you. When you submit to God's authority and that of godly leadership, you are secured and protected.

The three Hebrew children in Babylon were protected and shielded from the destructive power of the fiery furnace because of their submission to God. They would rather die than to worship and bow down to a graven image (Acts 3). Daniel submitted to God and the lions could not hurt him (Dan. 6). Peter submitted to God and God sent His angel to bring him out of the prison and deliver him from the expectation of Herod and elders of Israel. All the iron gates shut against him opened of their own accord to him (Acts 12). That was the power of submission at work. When you also submit to God, this great and supernatural power will work in your life, home and organization.

CHAPTER SIX

THE POWER OF SUBMISSION IN ELISHA

"So he departed from there, and found Elisha the son of Shaphat, who was plowing with twelve yoke of oxen before him, and he was with the twelfth. Then Elijah passed by him and threw his mantle on him. And he left the oxen and ran after Elijah, and said, "Please let me kiss my father and my mother, and then I will follow you." And he said to him, "Go back again, for what have I done to you?" So Elisha turned back from him, and took a yoke of oxen and slaughtered them and boiled their flesh, using the oxen's equipment, and gave it to the people, and they ate. Then he arose and followed Elijah, and became his servant." (1 Kings 19:19-21).

Elisha was a successful farmer when Prophet Elijah met him. He was actually working in his own farm, plowing with twelve yoke of oxen (a tractor in modern times) when Elijah threw his mantle upon him. Being a man of great understanding, Elisha recognized the divine authority that Elijah represented and gladly submitted under it. His quick response to a call into service was amazing. He neither argued nor protested or complained. He just arose and followed Elijah and became his servant. That is submission in its full colours.

From the day he accepted the call to be Elijah's servant, Elisha never looked back. He followed Elijah where ever he went. He waited upon him, served him faithfully, and protected his interests. Though there were many sons of the prophet under the leadership and authority of Elijah in those days, Elisha's submission was outstanding. Not only was he submissive to his master, he was also submissive to his parents. He regarded and respected them. When called into the service, he had just one request. He said to Elijah, **"Please let me kiss my father and my mother, and then I will follow you."** Obviously, Elisha held his parents in high esteem. He recognized their authority and treated them with utmost honour. What a lesson for our children today! Your parents must not be handled like rag, treated like pig and abandoned like thrash. If you do not honour and respect your parents, you are digging your own grave very early in life. The Bible commands: *"Children, obey your parents in the Lord, for this is right. "Honor your father and mother," which is the first commandment with promise: "that it may be well with you and you may live long on the earth." (Ephesians 6:1-3).*

SUBMISSION ATTRACTS GREATNESS

The way up is humility and service. Submission is the divine ladder to the top most top in life. People who recognize, respect and submit to authority are high flyers in life. Elisha submitted to Elijah and received double portion of his spirit. Those who had mocked and regarded him as stupid came back to bow before him. *"Now when the sons of the prophets who were from Jericho saw him, they said, "The spirit of Elijah rests on Elisha." And they came to meet him, and bowed to the ground before him." (2 Kings 2:15).*

Submission brings elevation but rebellion brings demotion. The Scripture admonishes: *"Humble yourselves in the sight of the Lord, and He will lift you up." (James 4:10).* When you are humble, accountable and submissive to the authority God has placed over you, your lifting is guaranteed. When you submit to the leadership and authority of your pastor in the church, the anointing for greatness will fall upon you, and you will stand out among the rest. When you obey orders and instructions of your boss in your office, you are due for promotion.

Elisha needed not to pray and fast for several months before the double portion of the anointing of Elijah rested upon him. All that he did was to serve Elijah in humility. You can not receive half the portion of the anointing upon your pastor or spiritual leader when you have not humbly and faithfully served him. Submission attracts divine impartation. Anointing does not flow into a proud and arrogant vessel. Many young ministers today are fasting and praying in vain seeking for divine impartation and empowerment. Let me tell you, true anointing answers only to submission. Submission is the channel through which the anointing and grace of God flows from your pastor to you. If submission is missing in your life, the anointing will be missing. You can not carry the anointing of the man of God you slander and gossip about in the secret. Don't be a fool. God is not mocked. It is what you sow that you will reap. If you sow the seed of humility, you will reap greatness.

Submission commands oil of greatness and excellence. It distinguishes you from your contemporaries. It sets you aside from the rest. It was this oil that set Elisha aside from the rest of the sons of the prophet and put him in the position of influence and authority. Until you know how to submit perfectly to authority, you cannot be lifted up to the position of authority. Many today are counting years on the same seat, the same office and the same spot, without being promoted because they are proud, arrogant and rebellious to higher authority. It takes a higher authority to promote you, so if you do not submit to a higher authority, you can never be in the position of authority. Do you desire greatness, promotion and excellence in life, the major pre-requisite is submission, faithfulness, humility, accountability, loyalty or integrity.

SUBMISSION BRINGS YOU BEFORE KINGS

Submission announces you and spreads your fame abroad. Humility is a pleasant but expensive fragrance or perfume; it goes before you and paves way for you. It endears you to great men. No kings or great men can tolerate proud and rebellious people around them. When the king of Israel, the king of Judah and the king of Edom needed a prophet to reveal God's mind to them, they sent for Elisha because of his profile. He was known as the man **"who poured water on the hands of Elijah." (2 Kings 3:11).** What announced and brought Elisha before the kings were not miracles, signs or wonders he had performed but his record of humble and faithful service under the leadership of Elijah. He was given access to the palace because his submission was evident to all. Submission is your license or access to the company of kings and great men.

Submission opens to you effective doors of opportunities. No wise businessmen will invest in a proud, arrogant and self-conceited person. No employer will invest their resources in an unruly staff that is full of himself and resents accountability. No great company will hire someone who is proud, arrogant and stubborn. No man will like to marry a woman who lacks good culture of respect and humility. No pastor will vouch for a rebellious and stubborn member of his church. Submission is the key which unlocks the doors of good job, favour, marriage, ministry and financial breakthrough. Adopt a lifestyle of submission from today and no good door will be shut against you. Submission is a good asset; go for it.

CHAPTER SEVEN

THE POWER OF SUBMISSION IN JOSEPH

"This is the history of Jacob. Joseph, being seventeen years old, was feeding the flock with his brothers. And the lad was with the sons of Bilhah and the sons of Zilpah, his father's wives; and Joseph brought a bad report of them to his father." (Genesis 37:2).

At the age of seventeen, Joseph had chosen the path of submission which eventually led him to the throne of a Prime minister in Egypt. Though very tough and challenging, Joseph shunned all distractions and temptations to turn away from the path of obedience to God. All throughout his pilgrimage, he remained steadfast, focused, humbled and devoted to God. Joseph's lifestyle of submission is indeed a challenge to every youth today.

SUBMISSION BIRTHS GREAT VISIONS

While feeding the flock with his brothers, Joseph refused to follow them to do evil. He would neither follow them to lie nor defraud their father. He stood for righteousness and would not compromise his principles in life. Rather than participating in his brothers' wickedness, Joseph contended with them and reported them to the authority – his father. ***"Those who forsake the law praise the wicked, But such as keep the law contend with them." (Proverbs 28:4).***

While in the house of Potiphar, Joseph was offered a free sex by an adulterous woman (his master's wife), but he declined and fled. Only a fool plays and toys with immorality. Joseph refused every invitation to rebellion and disobedience against God's word. Joseph protested: ***"There is no one greater in this house than I, nor has he kept back anything from me but you, because you are his wife. How then can I do this great wickedness, and sin against God?" (Genesis 39:9).***

As a result of Joseph's determination to keep the law of God and refusal to compromise with his wayward brothers and adulterous woman, God gave him great visions. He was chosen by God to be a saviour and deliverer in his generation. Submission to God and godly leadership opens your spiritual eyes to see visions of God. Rebellion will veil your mind and cast clouds of darkness upon your spiritual eyes. Submission creates a good spiritual atmosphere for the birth of great visions and ideas in your spirit and mind. Submission repels darkness from you, and gives you clarity of mind and purpose. Under a godly leadership, you will develop great insight and foresight.

> ***"Now Joseph had a dream, and he told it to his brothers; and they hated him even more. So he***

said to them, "Please hear this dream which I have dreamed: "There we were, binding sheaves in the field. Then behold, my sheaf arose and also stood upright; and indeed your sheaves stood all around and bowed down to my sheaf." And his brothers said to him, "Shall you indeed reign over us? Or shall you indeed have dominion over us?" So they hated him even more for his dreams and for his words. Then he dreamed still another dream and told it to his brothers, and said, "Look, I have dreamed another dream. And this time, the sun, the moon, and the eleven stars bowed down to me." (Genesis 37:5-9).

Not even the unbelief, hatred or conspiracy of Joseph's brothers could stop him from receiving great visions and dreams from heaven. He was connected to God of heaven via submission to His word, consequently, divine visions and ideas kept flowing to his spirit. When never anyone had difficult dreams or visions and became confused, they turned to Joseph for interpretation and clarity. When Pharaoh, the king of Egypt had dreams and became confused, Joseph was brought out of the prison, never to return there again.

Because Joseph remained under the authority of God's word, divine ideas and wisdom continually flowed into him. When all the people in his generation including the king became confused, Joseph was never confused. Submission eliminates confusion. Listening to the advice and wisdom of Joseph, Pharaoh said to his servants:

> *"Can we find such a one as this, a man in whom is the Spirit of God?" Then Pharaoh said to Joseph, "Inasmuch as God has shown you all this, there is no one as discerning and wise as you. "You shall be over my house, and all my people shall be ruled according to your word; only in regard to the throne will I be greater than you." And Pharaoh said to Joseph, "See, I have set you over all the land of Egypt." Then Pharaoh took his signet ring off his hand and put it on Joseph's hand; and he clothed him in garments of fine linen and put a gold chain around his neck. And he had him ride in the second chariot which he had; and they cried out before him, "Bow the knee!" So he set him over all the land of Egypt. Pharaoh also said to Joseph, "I am Pharaoh, and without your consent no man may lift his hand or foot in all the land of Egypt." And Pharaoh called Joseph's name Zaphnath-Paaneah. And he gave him as a wife Asenath, the daughter of Poti-Pherah priest of On. So Joseph went out over all the land of Egypt." (Genesis 41:37-45).*

Many believers today are living a life of confusion because they are living in defiance of God's word. Rebellion is the womb that births confusion. Many believers today are spiritually blind, walking in deep darkness, without a clear vision and direction in life. When Joseph submitted to God's authority, he received dreams, visions and interpretations from God. How can you receive great revelations and ideas when you disregard the authority of your husband? How will you not be confused when you don't treat your wife with dignity? How will you not be stranded in life, not knowing what to do with your life, when you are rebellious to your parents, guardians and mentors? How can God trust you with great visions and ideas when you despise, disrespect and disobey your pastor and spiritual leader?

SUBMISSION PRESERVES DESTINY

Submission shelters, secures and preserves your destiny in life. Recognizing, respecting and obeying godly leadership and authority provides a strong spiritual covering for your destiny. Though he was cast into the pit, sold into slavery and thrown into prison, Joseph's destiny could not be aborted. His dreams and visions in life came to pass in God-set time. Though Joseph's brothers stripped him of his coat of many colours which his father made for him, yet they could not strip him of his colourful destiny which God had ordained for him because of his heart of submission to God. In all his trials and temptations, Joseph remained faithful to God and his master, and so his dreams were preserved.

Rebellion is a destiny killer. It aborts and buries great dreams and visions. When you are not under a godly leadership, you are not under a divine covering and your destiny is not secured. No conspiracy, divination or enchantment against Joseph could drown or destroy his destiny because it was under the covering of God. Every opposition against his life became a stepping stone to his next position in life. His dreams could not be kept in the pit or the prison by any man or force in life because he was under the ultimate authority in life.

Though Joseph went from the pit into slavery and then into the prison, his destiny remained colourful, beautiful and glorious. God preserved Joseph's dreams and saw to it that they came to pass in the set time because of his absolute obedience and submission to the authority of God. In spite of all that his brothers planned and did against him and his dreams, his dreams still became a reality. At the end, his brothers bowed and fell down before him. ***"Then his brothers also went and fell down before his face, and they said, "Behold, we are your servants." (Genesis 50:18).***

Many great dreams and visions today are trapped in the pit and prison because of disobedience to God and godly leadership. It is only while you are under God-ordained authority that you can fulfill your God-ordained destiny. The authority you don't submit to can neither protect nor defend you. Submission is a spiritual shield that will protect your destiny against the fiery darts of the wicked. As long as you respect and obey the authority God has placed over you, there is no divination, spell or enchantment against your destiny that will prosper. However, rebellion is a spiritual cage or prison of potentials and destiny. Rebellion is the grave where dreams and visions are buried. The spirit of rebellion will swallow up your dreams. So, if you don't want your dreams or visions in life to descend into the grave and be swallowed up, break away today from the company of rebellious men. The Scripture warns that, *"He who walks with wise men will be wise, But the companion of fools will be destroyed." (Proverbs 13:20).* A wife who is rebellious and rude to her husband is foolish; keep no company with her lest she destroys your great marital dreams. A staff that is disobedient and arrogant to her boss is a fool, don't make friend with him lest he destroys your dreams to be great in life. A minister who disregard or discard the instructions and commands of his senior pastor is foolish, have nothing to do with him lest he destroys your dream of making heaven.

CHAPTER EIGHT

THE POWER OF SUBMISSION IN DAVID

"Now the LORD said to Samuel, "How long will you mourn for Saul, seeing I have rejected him from reigning over Israel? Fill your horn with oil, and go; I am sending you to Jesse the Bethlehemite. For I have provided Myself a king among his sons." And Samuel said, "How can I go? If Saul hears it, he will kill me." And the LORD said, "Take a heifer with you, and say, 'I have come to sacrifice to the LORD.' "Then invite Jesse to the sacrifice, and I will show you what you shall do; you shall anoint for Me the one I name to you." So Samuel did what the LORD said, and went to Bethlehem. And the elders of the town trembled at his coming, and said, "Do you come peaceably?" And he said, "Peaceably; I have come to sacrifice to the LORD. Sanctify yourselves, and come with me to the sacrifice." Then he consecrated Jesse and his sons, and invited them to the sacrifice. So it was, when they came, that he looked at Eliab and said, "Surely the LORD'S anointed is before Him." But the LORD said to Samuel, "Do not look at his appearance or at the height of his stature,

because I have refused him. For the LORD does not see as man sees; for man looks at the outward appearance, but the LORD looks at the heart." So Jesse called Abinadab, and made him pass before Samuel. And he said, "Neither has the LORD chosen this one." Then Jesse made Shammah pass by. And he said, "Neither has the LORD chosen this one." Thus Jesse made seven of his sons pass before Samuel. And Samuel said to Jesse, "The LORD has not chosen these." And Samuel said to Jesse, "Are all the young men here?" Then he said, "There remains yet the youngest, and there he is, keeping the sheep." And Samuel said to Jesse, "Send and bring him. For we will not sit down till he comes here." So he sent and brought him in. Now he was ruddy, with bright eyes, and good-looking. And the LORD said, "Arise, anoint him; for this is the one!" Then Samuel took the horn of oil and anointed him in the midst of his brothers; and the Spirit of the LORD came upon David from that day forward. So Samuel arose and went to Ramah. (1 Samuel 16:1-13).

SUBMISSION ENTHRONES BUT REBELLION DETHRONES

The passage above clearly reveals that God does not see as men see; men look at the face and outward appearance but God look at the heart. Before God will enthrone or promote any man, He will check what is in his heart. God is always looking for men who have the spirit of submission to enthrone and promote in life. God does not consider your stature but your spirit before He sets you on the throne of Glory in life. When God visited the house of Jesse, he found the spirit of humility and submission in David, and released upon him the oil of greatness in the midst of his brothers. Submission commands the release of oil of greatness.

Saul was the first king of Israel but when he chose a lifestyle of disobedience and rebellion, God dethroned him. When God commanded Saul to wipe out the Amalekites, sparing nothing; Saul disobeyed. He spared the king of Amalek and the best of the sheep, the oxen, the fatlings, the lambs, and all that was good (1 Sam. 15:1-9). *"Now the word of the LORD came to Samuel, saying, "I greatly regret that I have set up Saul as king, for he has turned back from following Me, and has not performed My commandments." And it grieved Samuel, and he cried out to the LORD all night." (1 Samuel 15:10-11).*

When you disobey the word of God, you grieve the heart of God. When you speak and work against your pastor, it grieves his heart. When you as a wife slander and disrespect your husband, you are causing him pains and grief. When you as a child dishonour your parents or guardian, you are causing them much pain. And according to the law of God, you will reap in abundance whatever you sow in life. ***"Do not be deceived, God is not mocked; for whatever a man sows, that he will also reap." (Galatians 6:7).*** This is the reason why many today are bound by the spirit of sorrow and pain. You cannot have joy when you cause pain or sorrow for others. How can you have peace and joy when you cause your parents or in-law pain and sorrow? How can you experience peace and joy when you sow the seed of discord and strife among the brethren through gossips, rumours and lies? When Saul grieved the heart of God and Samuel, a distressing spirit from the LORD troubled him (1 Sam. 16:14).

David was a man who highly esteemed authority. Even though God had rejected and forsaken Saul and had chosen and anointed David in his stead, yet David would neither say nor do any evil against Saul. Though Saul hated him and hunted for his life, yet David sought the good of Saul all the days of his life. Though Samuel had anointed him, yet David respected and submitted to the leadership of King Saul. Though he was the one who slain Goliath – a national threat, and all the women sang his praises, yet David remained humble and submissive to his master. He would have planned and staged a coup against King Saul, and usurped the throne, but David respected, honoured and obeyed the king's commands till God took him out of the way. This is submission in its true sense. What a challenge today to young ministers who become impatient, arrogant and independent because of a small measure of anointing God placed upon them to test them.

While Saul was still pursuing and hunting for David, the LORD delivered him into the hand of David, but David spared him. What a surprise! All the people with David urged him to kill the King so that he would immediately become the king, but David refused to be pushed against his master. He would not do any evil against the anointed of God. Can you now see why God chose to enthrone David and declared that he was a man after His own heart? The Bible testifies:

> *"Now it happened, when Saul had returned from following the Philistines, that it was told him, saying, "Take note! David is in the Wilderness of En Gedi." Then Saul took three thousand chosen men from all Israel, and went to seek David and his men on the Rocks of the Wild Goats. So he came to the sheepfolds by the road, where there was a cave; and Saul went in to attend to his needs. (David and his men were staying in the recesses of the cave.) Then the men of David said to him, "This is the day of which the LORD said to you, 'Behold, I*

will deliver your enemy into your hand, that you may do to him as it seems good to you.'" And David arose and secretly cut off a corner of Saul's robe. Now it happened afterward that David's heart troubled him because he had cut Saul's robe. And he said to his men, "The LORD forbid that I should do this thing to my master, the LORD'S anointed, to stretch out my hand against him, seeing he is the anointed of the LORD." So David restrained his servants with these words, and did not allow them to rise against Saul. And Saul got up from the cave and went on his way. David also arose afterward, went out of the cave, and called out to Saul, saying, "My lord the king!" And when Saul looked behind him, David stooped with his face to the earth, and bowed down. And David said to Saul: "Why do you listen to the words of men who say, 'Indeed David seeks your harm'? "Look, this day your eyes have seen that the LORD delivered you today into my hand in the cave, and someone urged me to kill you. But my eye spared you, and I said, 'I will not stretch out my hand against my lord, for he is the LORD'S anointed.' "Moreover, my father, see! Yes, see the corner of your robe in my hand! For in that I cut off the corner of your robe, and did not kill you, know and see that there is neither evil nor rebellion in my hand, and I have not sinned against you. Yet you *hunt my life to take it. "Let the LORD judge between you and me, and let the LORD avenge me on you. But my hand shall not be against you. "As the proverb of the ancients says, 'Wickedness proceeds from the wicked.' But my hand shall not be against you. "After whom has the king of Israel come out? Whom do you pursue? A dead dog? A flea? "Therefore let the LORD be judge, and judge between you and me, and see and plead my case, and deliver me out of your hand." (1 Samuel 24:1-15).*

SUBMISSION ESTABLISHES YOUR DOMINION

Submission does not only enthrone it also establishes on the throne. A submissive spirit will not only promote you, it will also sustain you in your exalted position. The greatest challenge in life is not getting to the top but staying on the top. Humility will not only lift you up, it will also keep you up; for God gives more grace to the humble. It takes more grace to stay up than to get up in life. When your submission to God and human leadership is in place, your dominion is in place. Submission is a stabilizer; it will keep your feet from sliding off the ladder of success and greatness in life.

The throne of Saul and his dominion over Israel would have been established but his disregard for spiritual authority prevented it. He despised the office of the prophet and took over the role and position of Samuel, and God took the kingdom from him. Here is the account of his disrespect for God's prophet:

> *"Then the Philistines gathered together to fight with Israel, thirty thousand chariots and six thousand horsemen, and people as the sand which is on the seashore in multitude. And they came up and encamped in Michmash, to the east of Beth Aven. When the men of Israel saw that they were in danger (for the people were distressed), then the people hid in caves, in thickets, in rocks, in holes, and in pits. And some of the Hebrews crossed over the Jordan to the land of Gad and Gilead. As for Saul, he was still in Gilgal, and all the people followed him trembling. Then he waited seven days, according to the time set by Samuel. But Samuel did not come to Gilgal; and the people were scattered from him. So Saul said, "Bring a burnt offering and peace offerings here to me." And he offered the burnt offering. Now it happened, as soon as he had finished presenting the burnt offering, that Samuel came; and Saul went out to meet him, that he might greet him. And Samuel said, "What have you done?" And Saul said, "When I saw that the people were scattered from me, and that you did not come within the days appointed, and that the Philistines gathered together at*

Michmash, "then I said, 'The Philistines will now come down on me at Gilgal, and I have not made supplication to the LORD.' Therefore I felt compelled, and offered a burnt offering." And Samuel said to Saul, <u>"You have done foolishly. You have not kept the commandment of the LORD your God, which He commanded you. For now the LORD would have established your kingdom over Israel forever.</u> "But now your kingdom shall not continue. The LORD has sought for Himself a man after His own heart, and the LORD has commanded him to be commander over His people, because you have not kept what the LORD commanded you." (1 Samuel 13:5-14).

Unlike Saul, David walked humbly with God and his throne was established forever. When David led the children of Israel to bring up the ark of God from the house of Obed-Edom to the City of David, it was said of David that he danced with all his might to the extent that his wife – Michal despised him. She said to David, ***"How glorious was the king of Israel today, uncovering himself today in the eyes of the maids of his servants, as one of the base fellows shamelessly uncovers himself!"*** But David replied, ***"It was before the LORD, who chose me instead of your father and all his house, to appoint me ruler over the people of the LORD, over Israel. Therefore I will play music before the LORD. "And I will be even more undignified than this, and will be humble in my own sight.***

But as for the maidservants of whom you have spoken, by them I will be held in honor." Therefore Michal the daughter of Saul had no children to the day of her death. (2 Samuel 6:20-23).

In response to the humility of David – how he humbled himself to dance with all his might before God and in the sight of all the children of Israel, God established his throne. God said to him, **"And your house and your kingdom shall be established forever before you. Your throne shall be established forever." (2 Samuel 7:16).** When a wife humbles herself before her husband, her seat and place in her home will be established for ever. Many women today are displaced from their marital homes because of their arrogance and insolence. How do you think you can keep the man you don't respect and obey? How will the wife you don't love, honour and respect desire to continue with you? Many marriages and homes have been shattered, destabilized and overthrown by the spirit of rebellion. Beware of rebellion! Your home, marriage, ministry or business is not established where the spirit of rebellion is in operation.

CHAPTER NINE

THE POWER OF SUBMISSION IN NAAMAN

"Now Naaman, commander of the army of the king of Syria, was a great and honorable man in the eyes of his master, because by him the LORD had given victory to Syria. He was also a mighty man of valor, but a leper. And the Syrians had gone out on raids, and had brought back captive a young girl from the land of Israel. She waited on Naaman's wife. Then she said to her mistress, "If only my master were with the prophet who is in Samaria! For he would heal him of his leprosy." And Naaman went in and told his master, saying, "Thus and thus said the girl who is from the land of Israel." Then the king of Syria said, "Go now, and I will send a letter to the king of Israel." So he departed and took with him ten talents of silver, six thousand shekels of gold, and ten changes of clothing. Then he brought the letter to the king of Israel, which said, Now be advised, when this letter comes to you, that I have sent Naaman my servant to you, that you may heal him of his leprosy. And it happened, when the king of Israel read the letter, that he tore his clothes and said,

"Am I God, to kill and make alive, that this man sends a man to me to heal him of his leprosy? Therefore please consider, and see how he seeks a quarrel with me." So it was, when Elisha the man of God heard that the king of Israel had torn his clothes, that he sent to the king, saying, "Why have you torn your clothes? Please let him come to me, and he shall know that there is a prophet in Israel." Then Naaman went with his horses and chariot, and he stood at the door of Elisha's house. And Elisha sent a messenger to him, saying, "Go and wash in the Jordan seven times, and your flesh shall be restored to you, and you shall be clean." But Naaman became furious, and went away and said, "Indeed, I said to myself, 'He will surely come out to me, and stand and call on the name of the LORD his God, and wave his hand over the place, and heal the leprosy.' "Are not the Abanah and the Pharpar, the rivers of Damascus, better than all the waters of Israel? Could I not wash in them and be clean?" So he turned and went away in a rage. And his servants came near and spoke to him, and said, "My father, if the prophet had told you to do something great, would you not have done it? How much more then, when he says to you, 'Wash, and be clean'?" So he went down and dipped seven times in the Jordan, according to the saying of the man of God; and his

flesh was restored like the flesh of a little child, and he was clean. And he returned to the man of God, he and all his aides, and came and stood before him; and he said, "Indeed, now I know that there is no God in all the earth, except in Israel; now therefore, please take a gift from your servant." (2 Kings 5:1-15).

SUBMISSION INITIATES RESTORATION

The passage above depicts the lifestyle of submission of Naaman and the power of submission to initiate healing and restoration. Naaman was a great and honourable man in the eyes of his master. Though a leper, yet he was the commander of the Syrian army and because of his submission to authority, God gave victories to Syria in battles. What a paradox! How a leper could lead an army to the war and yet had victory? That must be the LORD's doing. The Scripture affirms, **"because by him the LORD had given victory to Syria."** It was the LORD who gave the victory but He did it through Naaman – a leper. There must be something unique in Naaman that attracted God. That was nothing else but the spirit of submission.

Though Naaman was said to be a mighty man of valour and the commander of the Syrian army, yet he respected and operated under the authority of the King. Though a mighty man of valour, yet he listened to the counsel of his servant – a young girl taken as a captive from the land of Israel. When the young girl spoke in the hearing of Naaman, he did not just rise up to see Elisha the man of God. He rose up immediately to inform his master and seek for his approval. What a wise and submissive man. No wonder he was said to be a great and honourable man. ***"And Naaman went in and told his master, saying, "Thus and thus said the girl who is from the land of Israel." Then the king of Syria said, "Go now, and I will send a letter to the king of Israel."***

Naaman was a man who would neither do anything nor go anywhere unless his master approves of it. Though it was a personal matter, yet Naaman took it to his master. What a submissive man? No wonder the LORD was pleased be with him in the battle and won victory through him. Even when Naaman got to the land of Israel, he did not just go straight to the prophet but to the King of Israel. He respected and regarded the authority God has placed over the nation of Israel.

At first, Naaman was furious and went away angrily when the man of God did not come out to see him and performed the healing the way he had thought. However, because of his humility and submission, when his servants spoke to him, he listened and he went down and dipped himself seven times in the Jordan, according to the instructions of the man of God, and his flesh was restored like the flesh of a little child, and he was clean. Praise the LORD!

Naaman's journey to his healing and restoration revealed his heart of humility. He listened to a young girl's counsel, he sought permission from his master, he respected the King of Israel, and he listened to his servants, and obeyed the instructions of the man of God. The pathway to his restoration is the way of submission. He nearly turned back at the verge of his healing and restoration, but the spirit of submission prevented him. His servants spoke and he listened to them.

Beloved, how do you treat your master, boss, pastor, parents, servants or maids? The word or counsel you need to recover all that you have lost in life may be in the mouth of someone you least expected. Be very careful how you relate with those that are under your authority or lower to you. If Naaman did not treat the young girl well, she would not give him the counsel that resulted in his healing and restoration. If Naaman was not kind to his servants they would not have spoken to him and prevented him from walking away at the verge of his miracle.

Many believers today are still bound by the devil because of disregard for human leadership or authority. Naaman did not even know the God of Israel but he knew how to submit to those in power and authority. When he submitted to the man of God, it was counted for him as a submission to God. You can not claim to be under God's authority when you are not under a man's authority. God raises and sets men in position of authority so that there will be order in the home, school, society, church and nation. Where there is no leader there will be no order, and where there is no order, God will not show up. God hates confusion and confusion is the absence of order.

You don't need too many words or counsels to be great in life and recover all that the enemies have stolen from you. A word from the Lord is enough but you are not the one who determines the mouth piece that God will use to release the word into your life. Submission is powerful. It attracts the right words or counsels from God's mouth piece. Naaman's submission provoked the right counsel and instructions that led to his miracle. The way to your restoration is the way of humility and submission not only to God but also to godly authority. Despising and ignoring divine counsel is the sure way to remain in bondage and slavery. As great as Naaman was, he listened to his servants and he got his miracle. Submission is the master key that opens doors of restoration. In all your getting, make sure you get it.

CHAPTER TEN

THE POWER OF SUBMISSION IN NOAH

"And God said to Noah, "The end of all flesh has come before Me, for the earth is filled with violence through them; and behold, I will destroy them with the earth. "Make yourself an ark of gopherwood; make rooms in the ark, and cover it inside and outside with pitch. "And this is how you shall make it: The length of the ark shall be three hundred cubits, its width fifty cubits, and its height thirty cubits."You shall make a window for the ark, and you shall finish it to a cubit from above; and set the door of the ark in its side. You shall make it with lower, second, and third decks. "And behold, I Myself am bringing floodwaters on the earth, to destroy from under heaven all flesh in which is the breath of life; everything that is on the earth shall die. "But I will establish My covenant with you; and you shall go into the ark-you, your sons, your wife, and your sons' wives with you. "And of every living thing of all flesh you shall bring two of every sort into the ark, to keep them alive with you; they

shall be male and female. "Of the birds after their kind, of animals after their kind, and of every creeping thing of the earth after its kind, two of every kind will come to you to keep them alive. "And you shall take for yourself of all food that is eaten, and you shall gather it to yourself; and it shall be food for you and for them." Thus Noah did; according to all that God commanded him, so he did." (Genesis 6:13-22).

SUBMISSION SAVES FROM DESTRUCTION

Noah lived in a time when the earth was corrupt before God and filled with violence. In the midst of a corrupt generation, Noah's submission to God stands out. The Scriptures testifies of him: *"Noah was a just man, perfect in his generation. Noah walked with God." (Gen. 6:9).*

When the LORD saw that the wickedness of man was great in the earth and that every intent of the thoughts of his heart was only evil continually, the LORD was sorry that He had man on the earth and was grieved in His heart. *"So the LORD said, "I will destroy man whom I have created from the face of the earth, both man and beast, creeping thing and birds of the air, for I am sorry that I have made them." But Noah found grace in the eyes of the LORD." (Genesis 6:7-8).*

As revealed in out text, when God was set to destroy that

corrupt and violent generation which brought Him grief, God gave specific instructions to Noah. His deliverance and that of his family from the flood was tied to his total obedience and compliance with God's instructions and commands. In the midst of corrupt people, Noah obeyed and followed all the instructions that God gave to him. He made the ark according to God's specifications. He brought into the ark all that God commanded him to bring in. He entered and left the ark at God's command. Amidst scoffers and rebellious people, the Scripture declares: **"And Noah did according to all that the LORD commanded him." (Genesis 7:5).**

The same flood that destroyed the rebellious and corrupt generation lifted up Noah's ark, and it rose high above the earth (Gen. 7:17). While others were drowning and wailing, Noah and all those in the ark were cruising and feasting. By one man's submission to God's authority, his family and many living things were delivered from destruction. When a man submits to God, his family will be delivered from destructions. Submission to God delivers from death and destruction.

Noah's ark speaks of the following:

1. Salvation (Acts 4:12)
2. Grace (John 1:17)
3. Protection and divine security
4. The Word of God that was made flesh – to the level of

human comprehension, recognition and participation
5. The ark was both spiritual and physical. The physical body carries the spiritual body. 1Cor. 3:16, 1 John.4:4
6. Covenant (Gen. 6:18)
7. Healing and deliverance (Psa. 107:20)
8. Victory (1 John. 5:4-5)
9. Faith (Heb. 11:6)
10. Glory.

Noah's ark was born out of the following:

1. Righteousness
2. Hearing the word of God
3. Information. Lack of information initiates deformation. If you are not informed, you will be deformed.
4. Instructions. When you are instructed your future is secured.
5. Obedience and submission to God's commands
6. Faith and action. Action triggers manifestation resulting in satisfaction which leads to appreciation of God (Psa. 100, Gen. 8:20-22).
7. Power of choice and decision. Noah chose to be righteous in a perverse and corrupt generation. God gave instructions and Noah decided to obey, and he delivered his family and many living things from destruction.

Beloved, in the midst of this present corrupt and rebellious generation, you also can choose to submit to the word of

God and walk in righteousness. This wicked and perverse generation, like that of Noah, will also not go unpunished. God's flood of judgement is coming upon this generation of scoffers and unbelievers. But like Noah and his family, if you and your family come into the ark of obedience and submission to God, you will be spared in the day of judgement of the ungodly.

In this end time there is only one ark of salvation made and prepared for deliverance from the flood of sin, wickedness and judgement. This ark of salvation is neither a religion nor an institution, but a person. He is the Word who became flesh and dwelt among men many years ago. Like the Noah's ark, this end time's ark was born out of total submission to the will of God – the Father. God's ark of salvation for this generation upon whom the ends of the ages have come is JESUS CHRIST – THE SON OF GOD.

> *"Nor is there salvation in any other, for there is no other name under heaven given among men by which we must be saved." (Acts 4:12 NKJV)*

> *"Jesus said to him, "I am the way, the truth, and the life. No one comes to the Father except through Me. (John 14:6 NKJV)*
> *"For God so loved the world that He gave His only begotten Son, that whoever believes in Him should not perish but have everlasting life.*

"For God did not send His Son into the world to condemn the world, but that the world through Him might be saved.

"He who believes in Him is not condemned; but he who does not believe is condemned already, because he has not believed in the name of the only begotten Son of God."And this is the condemnation, that the light has come into the world, and men loved darkness rather than light, because their deeds were evil." (John 3:16-19 NKJV)

"Therefore we must give the more earnest heed to the things we have heard, lest we drift away. For if the word spoken through angels proved steadfast, and every transgression and disobedience received a just reward, how shall we escape if we neglect so great a salvation, which at the first began to be spoken by the Lord, and was confirmed to us by those who heard Him." (Hebrews 2:1-3 NKJV)

Beloved, as the LORD said to Noah, **"Come into the ark, you and all your household..."** God is calling you and your household today to come into Jesus Christ and be saved from all that is coming upon this evil generation. Noah obeyed God and so he was feasting when the wicked and rebellious people are wailing and mourning. If you also choose to submit to God's authority and godly leadership, when the wicked are groping in thick darkness, you will be marching in the light; when they are going down, you will be rising up; for your light has come has come and the glory of the LORD is risen upon you.

> *"For behold, the darkness shall cover the earth, And deep darkness the people; But the LORD will arise over you, And His glory will be seen upon you. The Gentiles shall come to your light, And kings to the brightness of your rising". (Isaiah 60:2-3 NKJV).*

www.ingramcontent.com/pod-product-compliance
Lightning Source LLC
Chambersburg PA
CBHW071536080526
44588CB00011B/1680